Rabbits

Rabbits

Sharon Sharth

THE CHILD'S WORLD®, INC.

Library of Congress Cataloging-in-Publication Data
Sharth, Sharon.
Rabbits / by Sharon Sharth.
p.   cm.
Includes index.
Summary: Introduces the physical characteristics,
behavior, habitat, and life cycle of rabbits.
ISBN 1-56766-587-X (lib. bdg. : alk paper)
1. Rabbits—Juvenile literature.
[1. Rabbits.]   I. Title.
QL737.L32S45   1999
599.32—dc21   98-30714
CIP
AC

Photo Credits

ANIMALS ANIMALS © Reed/Williams: 19
ANIMALS ANIMALS © Oxford Scientific Films: 20
© Art Wolfe/Tony Stone Images: 24
© Beth Davidow/WorldWild: 13
© Daniel J. Cox/Natural Exposures, Inc.: cover, 6, 9, 15, 30
© Gary Holscher/Tony Stone Images: 2
© 1993 George E. Stewart/Dembinsky Photo Assoc. Inc.: 23
© Joe McDonald: 10
© 1996 Rod Planck/Dembinsky Photo Assoc. Inc.: 26
© 1997 Rod Planck/Dembinsky Photo Assoc. Inc.: 29
© 1998 Rod Planck/Dembinsky Photo Assoc. Inc.: 16

On the cover...

Front cover: *Mountain cottontails* like this one like to hide in the tall grass.
Page 2: This *Netherland dwarf* rabbit is listening for danger.

Table of Contents

As you walk along a nature trail, you notice many things. High above, a bird chirps on a branch. As you look at the ground, you notice the grass moving in the distance. As you watch, two long, furry ears pop up out of the grass. A nose twitches as it sniffs the air. Then, quick as a wink, the little animal turns and bounds away. What was it? It was a rabbit!

⇐ This *eastern cottontail* is watching for danger.

What Are Rabbits?

Rabbits belong to a group of animals called **mammals.** Mammals have hair on their bodies and feed their babies milk from their bodies. Dogs, cows, and people are mammals, too.

Rabbits are covered with soft, fluffy hair. Even the bottoms of their feet are furry! This helps the rabbit grip onto ice and slippery rocks. Their powerful back legs help them to move and jump quickly. Their shorter front legs are used for digging and grooming. Many rabbits have a small, bushy tail, too. It looks like a bouncing cotton ball as the rabbit hops away!

This *whitetail jackrabbit* is resting just outside of its home. ⇒

Why Do Rabbits Have Such Big Ears?

A rabbit's ears are made to hear well. They are shaped like a funnel, which helps them catch all kinds of sounds—even ones people cannot hear! Each ear can turn in a different direction to pick up any noise that might mean danger.

The ears also help to keep the rabbit warm in the winter and cool in the summer. In hot weather, blood flows through the ears and is cooled by the air. During cold weather, less blood flows to the ears and the rabbit stays warm.

⇐ You can see the blood vessels in this *black-tailed jackrabbit's* ears.

Are There Different Kinds of Rabbits?

There are lots of different kinds, or **species,** of wild rabbits. The largest wild rabbit is the *Central African rabbit.* It weighs almost 7 pounds and is 20 inches long. The *pygmy rabbit* is the smallest rabbit in the world. It weighs only 9 ounces.

The most common rabbits in North and South America are *cottontails.* They can be found in almost every type of area—especially in places where they can find lots of food.

This *desert cottontail* is sitting in some tall grasses. ⇒

Where Do Rabbits Live?

Rabbits can be found in grassy meadows, mountains, desert areas, jungles, and swamp lands. Many rabbits live in large groups, too. Some rabbits make their homes by digging holes, or **burrows,** underground. This is where they sleep and give birth to their babies.

Most cottontails live above ground. They find shelter and make nests under bushes, in scooped-out places in the grass, or in other animals' burrows. They stay hidden most of the day. In the early morning and at dusk, the rabbits come out to feed and explore.

This mountain cottontail has made its home in a hollow log. ⇒

Rabbits are almost always hungry. They are planteaters, so they like to nibble on grasses, clover, daisies, and even crops. Rabbits are not very helpful to farmers. That is because they eat the soybeans, carrots, grains, and lettuce the farmers are trying to grow! In the winter, rabbits search for berries, roots, and twigs. They scrape and eat the bark from young trees, too.

⇐ Eastern cottontails like this one love to nibble on dandelions.

Rabbits have two kinds of teeth. Their front teeth, or **incisors,** are used for biting and cutting. These teeth never stop growing. In fact, rabbits need to chew on trees and twigs all the time to keep the teeth short. Their back teeth are flat and wide. They are used to grind and chew food.

You can easily see the incisors of this *mini French lop-ear.* ⇒

What Are Baby Rabbits Like?

A male rabbit is called a **buck.** A female rabbit is called a **doe.** After the buck and doe mate, the male leaves. The female returns to her den and prepares a soft nest of grass and fur that she plucks from her belly. One month later, about four or six baby rabbits, or **kits,** are born.

Rabbit kits are born blind and deaf. They also have no fur on their bodies. At first, the kits cannot eat plants like their mother. Instead, they drink milk from her body. After four weeks, the kits are strong enough to eat regular foods. They go off on their own and are ready to have their own kits in just a few months.

This baby eastern cottontail is staying safe by hiding in some flowers. ⇒

How Do Rabbits Stay Safe?

Rabbits have many enemies. In fact, many rabbits never get to be a year old. Eagles, hawks, and owls swoop down on rabbits from the sky. Foxes, bobcats, and dogs chase and attack rabbits on the ground. Snakes and weasels sneak into burrows and nests. And humans kill millions of rabbits every year for their fur, for food, or for sport.

Since they have so many enemies, rabbits have learned to be very careful. They rarely travel far from the safety of their homes. When they sense danger, rabbits scrunch down in the grass. Their fur often has colors or markings, called **camouflage,** that help them blend in with their surroundings.

Sometimes rabbits warn each other of danger. They bang on the ground with their back legs— "THUMP–THUMP–THUMP!" Then they run for cover. Often, rabbits escape into holes in the ground or into bushes or tall grasses. After the danger passes, the rabbits slowly come out of their hiding places.

This desert cottontail is standing tall as it listens for danger. ⇒

How Can You Learn About Rabbits?

You can learn a lot about rabbits just by watching them. If you know where to look, you can sometimes see rabbits eating in the early morning or evening. You can also follow a rabbit's tracks in the mud or snow. Brown, bare patches in grassy fields show where rabbits may have been eating. Look carefully. If you're quiet and still, you just might see a rabbit!

⟸ This mountain cottontail is resting in a green Montana forest.

Glossary

buck (BUK)
A buck is a male rabbit.

burrows (BUR–ohz)
Burrows are holes animals dig in the ground to create a home. Some rabbits live in burrows.

camouflage (KAM–oo–flazh)
Camouflage is special coloring or markings that help an animal hide. Many rabbits have camouflage.

doe (DOH)
A doe is a female rabbit.

incisors (in–SY–zerz)
Incisors are the teeth that a rabbit uses to bite and cut. A rabbit's incisors grow all the time.

kits (KITS)
Baby rabbits are called kits. Kits are born blind, deaf, and without any fur.

mammals (MA–mullz)
Mammals are animals that have hair and feed their babies milk from their bodies. Dogs, cows, and rabbits are all mammals.

species (SPEE–sheez)
A species is a different type of an animal. There are many different species of rabbits in the wild.

Index